Permanent Damage

Miles Gibson

Permanent Damage

Eyre Methuen

First published in 1973 by Eyre Methuen Ltd
11 New Fetter Lane London EC4P 4EE
Copyright © 1973 by Miles Gibson

Printed in Great Britain by
Redwood Press Ltd Trowbridge Wiltshire

SBN 413 29650 4 hardback
    413 29660 1 paperback

Acknowledgements
Some of these poems have appeared previously
in the following: *Amazing Grace, Poetry
Review, Resurgence, Ostrich, Tomorrow Magazine,
Wankers Cramp, Scrip* and the *Daily Telegraph
Magazine.*

Contents

Introduction

Hullo

Hullo

What are you doing?

I am commiting suicide

Does it hurt?

Not if you do it slowly

Duty

I am not unhappy
I have a wife
two children
a job with the general
insurance plan

I eat my cornflakes
I keep my shoes clean
I have no complaints

I am here
I have signed the forms
I have made the bed
I had a moustache
but I shaved it off

do not watch me
do not hurt me
do not ask me
who I am

I have a wife
two children
a job with the general
insurance plan

Fight

the head separates from the body
cuts loose
goes floating over rooftops
falls through a window
lands up in a jug

the arms strike out next
clench hands
elbow their way to the door
shake a fist at the street
punch back at the sky

the legs kick up at the trunk
put the boot in
dance on the ribcage
run from the bedroom
leap into the bath

fingers fall
from the sky
a chin wags
helpless from the jug
someone comes
to make a list
and starts to tidy up

The Consumers' Lament

we make the margarine
we sell the margarine
with margarine fingers
we glue up our mouths

in the papers
we read of atrocities
someone was murdered
someone was raped

with margarine outrage
we shake our heads
we wave our fists

a burst of applause
for the hero
some warm margarine
to spread on our grief

but something goes wrong
the news doesn't change

blood flows through the cinema doors
bombs crash through the radio
refugees pour from the television sets

waistdeep in margarine anger
we make our margarine protest
we write to the papers
we phone up the planners

it's all very upsetting
and children watching too

9

Ark

when the last button had surrendered
and the final zipper had been stormed
when the rain had stopped
and he was thankful for aftershave
and clean under pants
when the lady in the red lipstick
stopped complaining & opened her legs
a thousand animals
two by two poured
out of her body
like a conjurer's hat

well he wasn't expecting that
was he?
no
he wasn't expecting that

Owl One

he was so large that
no forest could contain him
he spent his life on
the branches of hell
staring
like a monk of doom

by night his moaning
haunted the world
but during the day
he threaded a necklace
from the skulls
of mice

when he died he fell
with a blow that wounded
the forests
his blood poisoned the rivers
and his bones stuck fast
in the throat of the earth

Owl Two

she dropped like a quince
through the lantern beam
of his ancient stare
and tore out his heart
with her gentleness

at first
he thought the end had come
he smelt of fear
and sometimes death
but later
when his nerves were strong
and she was happy
with his egg
they dwelt in a bucket
near the garden of eden
where they wove a great nest
from the sinews of mice

Owl Three

this one lived in a zoo
where darkness is measured
in inches and the mice
are enriched with
vitamin-plus

he was blind in one eye
and his talons were cut
but he was
content
in his way

at dusk
he turned his one eye in
ward flew through forests
of his birth where
secret as the root of pain
he feasted on
the blood of sheep
and the ancient songs
of the moon and the earth

Owl Four

there was once
an owl who lived in
bournemouth
in a damp brown hotel
with a view of the pier

he never had a visitor
and all his letters
were the kind that
offer sixpence off green soap

some said
he was a russian prince
while others heard
he'd lost his wife

one day they
found he'd hanged himself
with butcher's string
behind the shower

inside a jug they found
a foot
while inside the wardrobe
sat the head of a rat

Owl Five

in the space
between one question
and the next
an owl is sleeping
through a night of storms

her head is empty of dreams
and in their place
broods a single egg

proudly she cradles it
in a warm nest of rags
vainly she waits for it
listens for a sound within

what will emerge from this egg?
perhaps the eye of a cat
perhaps a hand in a sleeve
or just the sound of the rain
as it runs through the trees?

Roast Owl

1 large owl
½ lb dock leaves
¼ lb butter
small pot of blood

i   pluck and wash the owl clean
     remove beak and bind claws

ii   stuff with sorrow
     and a twist of leaves

iii brush with butter
     and a teaspoon of blood

iv   stand in moderate oven
     380 degrees or gas no 5

     serves one

Milky Owl Poultice

1 small town owl
1 cup mustard
3 eggs
milk
garlic
a length of thick string

   i   drown the owl in a pint of milk
          stuff with garlic
          wrap the head up in string

   ii   stir in mustard
          and a finger of egg

  iii   boil in a shallow bucket
          till the leg leaves the wing

  iv   apply to affected parts

Asylum

she walked to the end
of the only known world
and dropped off the edge
like a plum

when she woke up
her brains were bruised
bars appeared at the window
faces appeared at the bars

of course
they treat her kindly
where she's gone
on thursdays she has visitors
when large pale nurses
help her dress
they treat her kindly
and we
ourselves are not afraid

we can still open
or close doors
thread needles slice bread

and walk carefully

making sure that one foot
at least
is always on the ground

The Last Door

the first door of the dream
leads out
onto the roof of the world
— amazement
applause
and a signed guarantee
for eternal life

the second door leads
to the great book of answers
a scorecard a pencil
and a room full of leaves

beyond the third door
giant photographs
of beautiful girls
recordings of laughter
a test tube of tears

beyond the fourth door
rain
an armchair for the fifth
and so on
through the dream
the doors appear
the happy endings appear
in a giant queue

but the last door
is not like the rest
its colour is the shadow of ashes
its lock is the size of a fist

this one then
must never be opened

for behind this door
a scratched film of your own self
endlessly playing you
locked in a room
on the edge of the day
      forever and ever waking alone

Hero

even before he was born
the people were waiting
his first words were recorded
in a dozen tongues
and his birthplace
laid open to visitors

every movement he made
he made for the world
every action was recorded
and applauded as news

when he turned his head
the wind changed direction
when he combed his hair
a million extra combs were sold

he rewrote every book
he refought every war
and if the laws disagreed
he changed them

when he died
they raised him a tomb
in a car park as big
as the end of the world

the people wept
the sky brightened
and somewhere a blackbird
started to sing

The Three Graces

I.

here is a poet
who holds his pencil clumsy as a rifle butt

inside his head
rest monotonies of raped women

vinegar stains his lips
at his side hang cripple pelts

his poems gasp like obscene phone calls
at night he dreams of pillows stuffed with flowers

he is very unhappy

2.

here is a poet
who folds his poems in the shape of wings

inside his head
great winds thrash through canvas doors

he flaps pages through the air
scales the words like a ladder of foam

his poems collapse in a mess of bruises
at night he dreams of pillows stuffed with flowers

he is very unhappy

3.

here is a poet
who lets his pen draw a face on his thumb

he does not even like poetry
he prefers girls and black cigarettes

he is too busy
he gets someone else to write his poems

this someone works hard
writes careful pillows stuffed with flowers

at night he dreams of rape and flight
he is very unhappy

The Smile

It is simple.

A man is sitting in bed. It is afternoon.

There is a cupboard by the bed. A cupboard, a
table and a single chair. There are clothes on the
carpet, flowers on the cupboard. Tulip. Iris. On the
chair a single shoe.

The man sitting in bed wears blue pyjamas. He
starts to smile. The smile pushes out against his
mouth and folds up his eyes. It is a confident smile.
A decisive smile. He believes it to consider all things.
He believes it to consider the bed, the afternoon
and the smell of death that escapes from his teeth.
He believes it to consider other rooms even, other
lives. For a while he remains motionless. He is
building the smile up. Adding to it, polishing the
shallow curve, strengthening the arch with proof of
itself. For a while he remains motionless, aiming
the smile at a spot on the chair.

Sitting next to the man, a girl. She does not wear
blue pyjamas. Nor does she smile. Instead the girl
presses a corner of the sheet against her mouth and
weeps. Hair sticks to her face with this weeping.
Her knuckles are white and wet with it. Her face
has collapsed into the disaster of it. This weeping
is also confident but it considers nothing. It believes
only in its own sorrow.

At last the man shifts a little. He puts his arm
around the girl and presents her with the finished
smile. It is a smile of astounding confidence. As if
he were about to solve the problem of life itself. As

24

if all the peoples of the world had gathered at the
window to cheer him on. The girl turns her misery
towards him. She buries her face into the blue
pyjamas. She stops weeping. She stops sobbing.
She grows very still. The peoples of the world break
into thunderous applause. Life crawls into a ditch
and drowns. The man modifies the smile to include
patience, modesty, sympathy and love. Pinches the
corners. Adjusts the lower lip. More applause. More
drowning. It is a remarkable success.

And now you yourself. Yes. What is your name?
What is your despair.

Elijah

A man walks to a car.

He is so old this man that the sunlight grazes him.
His skin shines like wet paper and his veins pump
through like string. He is so old that every step is a
rattle of angry nerves. Every breath is a rustle of
pain.

But he reaches the car. He stretches out a crumpled
arm, he unfolds a knot of fingers and touches the
door.

It is so new this car that the sunlight pours off it
like water. Whole choirs sing from the engine and
the tail lights spit flame. The exhaust is wide as a
drain. The boot as big as a tomb.

The old man climbs into the driving seat of this car
and closes the door. He turns the key in the
dashboard. He turns on the choirs and lets out the
clutch.

And as he drives off the whole road lights up. As
far as the eye can see the road lights up. On the
horizon a deep glow appears. Angels reach for their
songbooks, beautiful women start to wave from
the curb. The road starts to curve and point up at
the sky.

Grandma

they clean out her wrinkles with a small knife
with a file they work on her gums and her teeth
next they pad the body with rags
breasts are built
here and there a suggestion of fat
someone brings in a blowtorch
a twinkle is added to the eye
a glow to the cheeks
then they carry her down the steps
to the waiting crowds
they lift her shoulder high
they show her to the mothers
they show her to the children
they distribute balloons and small cakes
everyone loves the family

Portrait

on a canvas
eight feet by twelve
the colour of bones
the varnish of flesh

before the canvas
an old man who sits
who sits and waits
for the flinch
of a brushstroke
the movement of space

who waits
till the canvas bursts
till the colours
run grey

till the varnish
explodes
and coats him in ashes

who waits
till he himself
is the canvas
till he himself
is a brushstroke

till he himself
is nothing at all

Dream

he dreams a dream
every night the same dream
the drums roll
the heads roll
the poison wails
against the sky

tonight he wakes up
makes himself tea
and lights a cigarette
tonight something's gone wrong

tonight from behind the curtain
he peers into the street
where the drummer already
looks up at the sky

and there
he is caught

not yet awake
no longer asleep
rolling down the gutter
of his dream
into the sewer of circumstance

Glass

1

your smile is a fist of shadows
    stitched to my wall

your hair
is a smudge of darkness
    left in my room

I touch your embrace
    your perfume poisons me

I ask you for nothing
    you cannot hear me

    my hands
thread your spine
    with promises

2

in a small box
    I have collected your kisses

across my arm
    your folded glances

you ask me for nothing
    I cannot hear you

    your tears
scratch my face
    with promises

Ghost

at daybreak
your smile is the first to go
next your breasts
whose warmth I cannot reconstruct
escape my hands disguised as fists

your arms already incomplete
no longer meet towards embrace
an elbow fades and now a wrist
as though you stood some distance off
and beckoned back these hoarded shapes

you are about to leave now for the last time

I have tried to remember everything
your movements laugh our common pain
I have tried to retain you
clutching memories as one attempting
to enter his own shadow
I have tried to restore you
yet wake these mornings
knowing well that each new light
steals something new

Fragments from a page of instructions for survival

One

disguise yourself
as a lightweight suit

skin for the jacket
bones for the buttons

keep your tongue
in a trouser pocket

hang yourself
on a stout green peg

Two

shut yourself in a small red box
nail down the lid
and turn out the light

next start a scream
scream until another scream answers

never leave your box
in emergency eat your thumbs

Three

take a knife
cut yourself into thin strips
stand on a corner
hand yourself out to passers by

Four

gather up your footprints
climb into yourself

extinguish your eyes
screw down your jawbone

spit earth in your ears
lest familiar voices prise you out

next search for footholds
in the seam of your ribcage

crawl up your spine
till you slip off the edge

Five

comb your hair
smile at the person next to you
keep smiling
smile until the smile is returned
never leave this person
use the smile as evidence

Six

save all traces of yourself
burn them
swallow the ashes

Seven

find a word
memorize it
go into the world
meet someone
exchange words
take this word
exchange it for another word
repeat
repeat and repeat
repeat until your word is returned

Eight

1. using a black pen
    print this poem
    carefully across your face

2. work in block capitals
    start at the brow
    and move down to the chin

3. place the finished head
    in a plastic bag

4. set fire to it

Nine

draw a picture of your own death
hang it on the wall
spend your life ignoring it

Tree

on the top branch
sits a naked man
bruised with wind
and hugely alone

on the branches below
squat impossible dreams
the half-ape-mad
and the not-yet-man

beneath them
laze the true ape
and the true monkey

directly below
comes the lemur
and at the bottom of the tree
on the last branch of all
hangs the skull of a shrew

from somewhere called distance
a spike of rain arrives
and punches out the hood of leaves

someone sniffs the air
someone rattles his teeth
someone yawns
someone shouts
look out behind you

the man screams
falls off

everybody
moves up one

Complaint

I phoned
and told them that my wife
was being eaten
by the bath

they held their silence
for a while
and then they shouted
phone Complaints

I phoned
and told them that my wife
was being eaten
by the bath

they said
we're only open Tuesdays
        if you have to
phone us then

I phoned
and told them that my wife
had just been eaten
by the bath

they said
        make sure the hair
won't clog the plughole
flush the main pipes
scrub the drain

Night

when suddenly
a knuckle of rain
bruises the street

the disembowelled day
is wrapped
in tarpaulins of shadow
and slipped in the river

fog tramples eastward

the moon starts to bark

Permanent Damage

Step One

a red jug
on a black table
beside the jug
a white plate
on the plate
a wedge of cheese

positively
that is all

from a small window
beside the table
sunlight settles
in the room

the cheese
sweats in concentration
at the base of its neck
the jug
stops a yawn

nothing
moves

Step Two

a table
a cupboard
a row of white chairs

but this time
something
goes wrong

beneath the table
something like a spine
crawls out

inside the cupboard
fingers find
a disused head

teeth screw into sockets
bone clips onto bone

something goes wrong

something sits up
and looks around
something like history
something like justice

something saddles the chairs
something like terror
something like man

the table winces
the cupboard screams

someone's busy being born

Step Three

i

on a piece of slate we work out the facts
the dreams that are true
the dreams that are not

we calculate the speed of mountains
weighing one cloud against the next

we divide
we subtract

but it doesn't add up

ii

we make more calculations
distances are measured
morals are deduced

someone
must have
made a mistake

iii

on a small hill the argument grows

someone loses a ribbon of muscle
someone tears out a cushion of flesh

a decimal point turns the colour of blood

iv

later there is only silence

we gather the bones in a great pit
we listen to the silence

but what does it mean
where is the proof
nobody knows

more slate is needed

Step Four

i

this time we are more cautious
we find ourselves sun
and a patch of damp earth

we space out in the earth
we plant ourselves carefully
standing in rows

we concentrate

we study the bushes
we point at the sun

and here a foot takes slender root
and now the promise of a leaf

ii

but it is not enough
we must plant deeper

iii

we hollow out the earth
we plant ourselves deeper

we cover our heads
we dream the sleep of orchid bulbs

iv

time passes
the rains come

the earth grows warm
but we do not move
we who dream the sleep of bulbs

we do not move
we lie very quiet
without even a shoot

Step Five

i

but sometimes there is only water

ii

we bend to drink the water
watching ourselves
in the bright reflection

soon we grow afraid
we try to hide in the water
throw off ourselves
and take a water disguise

we sit at the bottom
odourless fireproof
believing ourselves water soluble

iii

but it doesn't last
there are the complaints
the doubts

we push up again
breaking water with angry lungs
the surface mends
our faces return

iv

this happens for weeks
for months
for as long as there are faces
for as long as there is water

many people drown

Step Six

i

at a quarter past three
in the afternoon
a trickle of sand starts
to fall from the wall

a little plaster falls away
dust and the smell of bricks

ii

towards evening
the hole first appears

iii

not the sort of hole through
which landscapes are seen

not the sort of hole
through which one sticks a thumb
whistles or blows

not the cavity
in the tooth of wisdom
or the crack in the castle gate

but a round and perfect hole
entirely filled with itself
entirely closed to the world

iv

the hole grows

v

grows
till the wall itself is the hole
and the hedge behind the wall
and the street behind the hedge
till the town itself is the hole
grows
till the sky is bleached hollow
till the earth is drained white

vi

take a pencil
go out in the world
mark where the hole begins
mark where the hole ends

Leisure

what shall we do now

what shall we do
while we wait
for the war to break
the rain to come
the joke to go bad

what shall we do
now the factory is closed
and machines fill the air
with their sermons at night

what shall we do
now the work is all done
and we wait for the poison
to sink to our feet

lets complain
about the price of eggs
lets start a march
and fight in the street
lets take our shirts off
and fly to the sun

lets form a queue
and wait

Tailpiece

but it enters the room
without knocking
sinks into the wallpaper
fixes you with a yellow eye

at first you fold shirts
into a small bag
change your address
sleep in your clothes

later you stop running
you sleep exhausted
in a nettlepatch of nerves
waiting for the tremble to stop
for the boot to go in
waiting for the gasp of pain
for the flutter of death

but nothing is certain

you move towns
you change jobs
you grow old painfully